BRASS IN COLOR

Beginner Method Series

FRENCH HORN

LESSON BOOK THREE

by Sean Burdette

Illustrations by
David Ore, BLUE ASTER STUDIO
Bloomington, IN

ISBN 13: 978-1-949670-06-6
Copyright © 2019 BRASS IN COLOR, LLC
All Rights Reserved.

Any duplication, adaptation or arrangement of the compositions, tablature design and illustrations contained in this collection and series requires the written consent of the publisher. Unauthorized uses are an infringement of the U.S. Copyright Act and are punishable by law.

Introduction

French Horn Book Three of the Brass in Color Beginner Method Series uses a color-coded tablature (Color Fingerings) to help students learn the fingerings of the French horn and apply them to notes in the High Range.

The High Range begins with the notes A♭/G♯ notated on the staff, and the remaining notes of the High Range are presented in an ascending chromatic order and end with the note **C** that is also notated on the staff. Along with the notes of the High Range the notes of the Middle Range are also presented in an ascending order to help students learn the correct fingerings for the High Range.

While learning the notes of the High Range students will be introduced to the music concepts of playing in 3/4 time, dotted quarter notes and the harmonic minor scale. Additionally, etudes are included to complete this French horn instructional series. These etudes allow students to practice playing each pitch of the Low, Middle and High Ranges without using Color Fingerings.

Standard music notation has also been included with each lesson. Breath marks, articulation, dynamics and tempi are not noted in the lessons and may be added by the instructor as needed. Also, key signatures are not used so that students will focus primarily on listening and learning the fingerings associated with the notes.

This beginner method series for French horn also has a companion website:

BRASS IN COLOR (www.brassincolor.com)

On the website you will find audio for each lesson as well as different activities, videos and other resources to help students learn to play the French horn.

Contents

Lesson 1	4
Lesson 2	6
Technique Exercises 1	8
Technique Exercises 2	10
Songs Group 1	12
Songs Group 2	14
Lesson 3	16
Technique Exercises 3	18
Songs Group 3	20
Songs Group 4	22
Lesson 4	24
Technique Exercises 4	26
Songs Group 5	28
Songs Group 6	30
Lesson 5	32
Technique Exercises 5	34
Songs Group 7	36
Songs Group 8	38
Songs Group 9	40
Etudes	42
Music Definitions and Symbols	44
Fingering Chart	45

Lesson 1

2nd and 3rd Valves

For this fingering you press down the second and third valves. This is the fingering you use to play the notes A♭/G♯ in the High Range. It is the same fingering you use to play the notes A♭/G♯ in the Low Range. (This fingering is not used for notes in the Middle Range.)

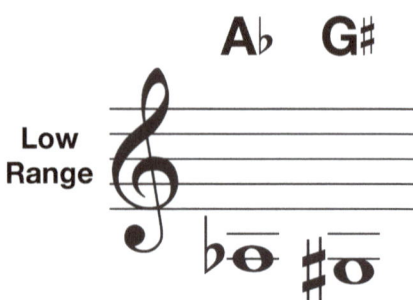

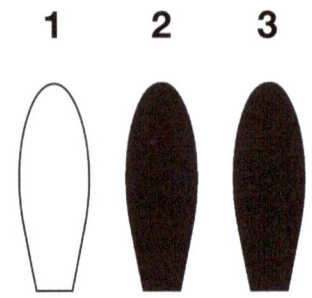

Play by Listening

Listen to the following exercises. Use the Color Fingerings to play what you hear.

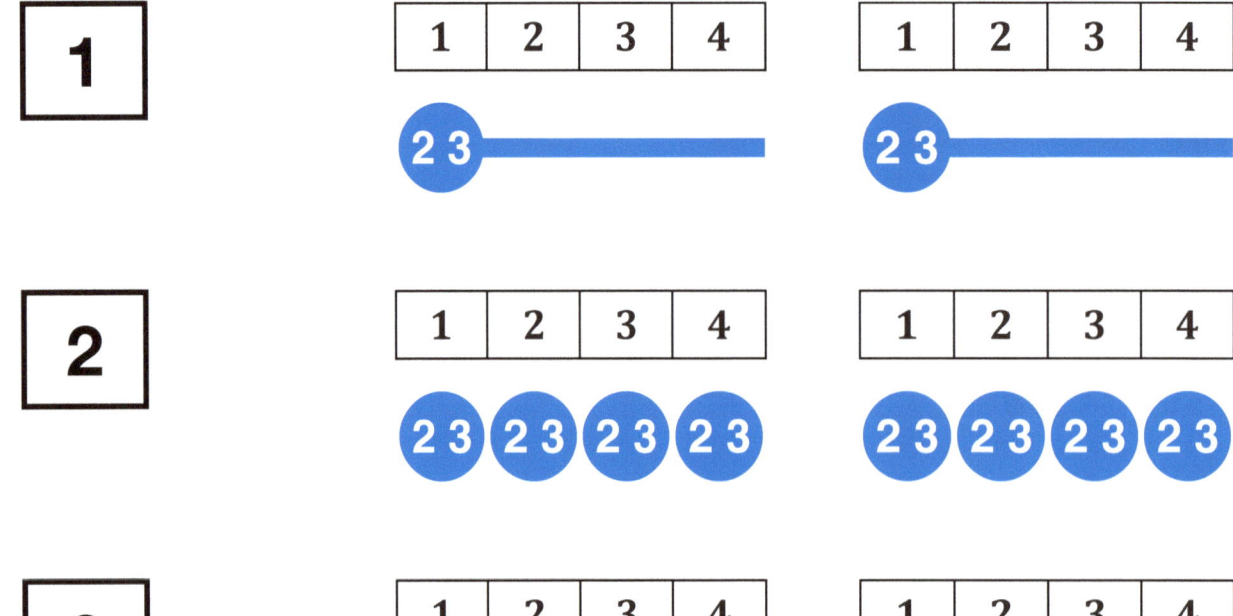

Lesson 1

Going Up, Up and Up

The chart below shows the Color Fingerings for each pitch of the Middle Range and how these fingerings are used to play each pitch of the High Range. The Middle Range is arranged in an ascending order (going up) beginning with the notes **C♯/D♭** and ending with the note **G**. In music notation the highest note of the Middle Range (**G**) comes before the lowest notes of the High Range (**G♯/A♭**).

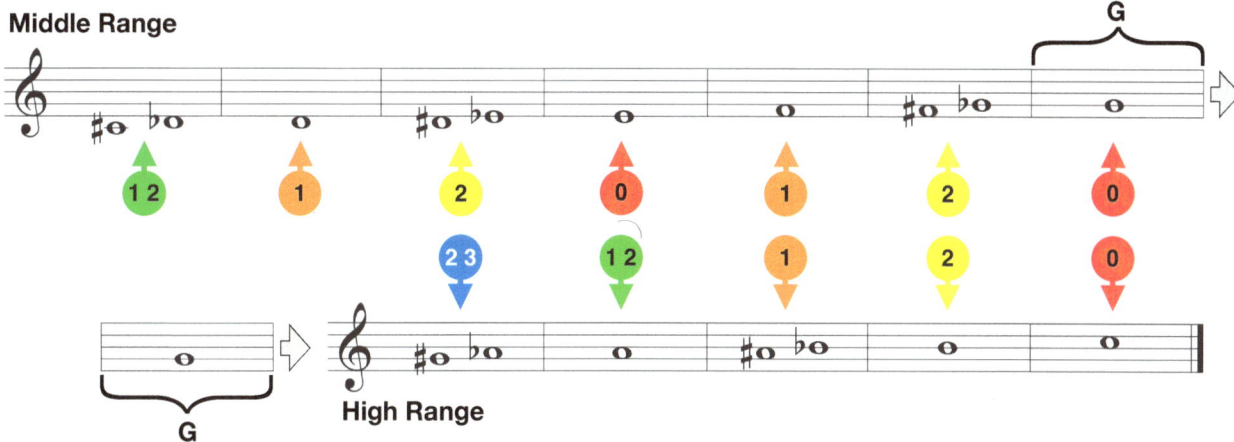

Play by Reading

Play the following exercises reading music notation.

★ **A♭** and **G♯** are written differently, but they sound the same.

Brass in Color

Lesson 2

1st and 2nd Valves

For this fingering you press down the first and second valves. This is the fingering you use to play the note **A** in the High Range. It is the same fingering you use to play the notes **D♭/C♯** in the Middle Range.

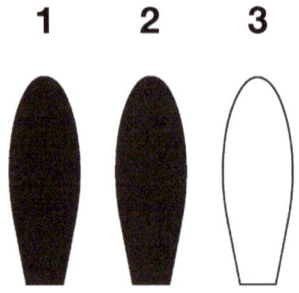      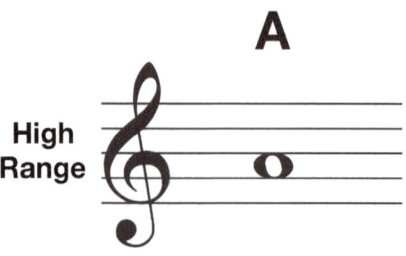

Play by Listening

Listen to the following exercises. Use the Color Fingerings to play what you hear.

Lesson 2

3/4 Time Signature

In French Horn Book One you learned about the 4/4 time signature and how this music symbol tells you how many beats are in a measure and which rhythm value (quarter note, half note or whole note) is given the beat. When you have a 3/4 time signature the quarter note falls on the beat, and there are 3 beats to a measure. (Note: In a time signature the lower number represents the rhythm value that gets the beat and the upper number represents the number of beats in each measure.)

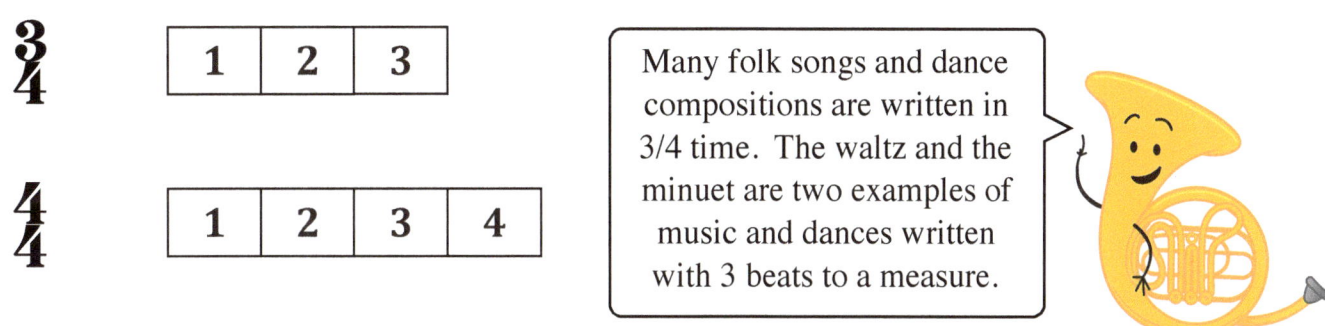

Many folk songs and dance compositions are written in 3/4 time. The waltz and the minuet are two examples of music and dances written with 3 beats to a measure.

Play by Reading

Play the following exercises reading music notation.

Brass in Color

Technique Exercises 1

Play by Listening

Listen to the following exercises. Use the Color Fingerings to play what you hear.

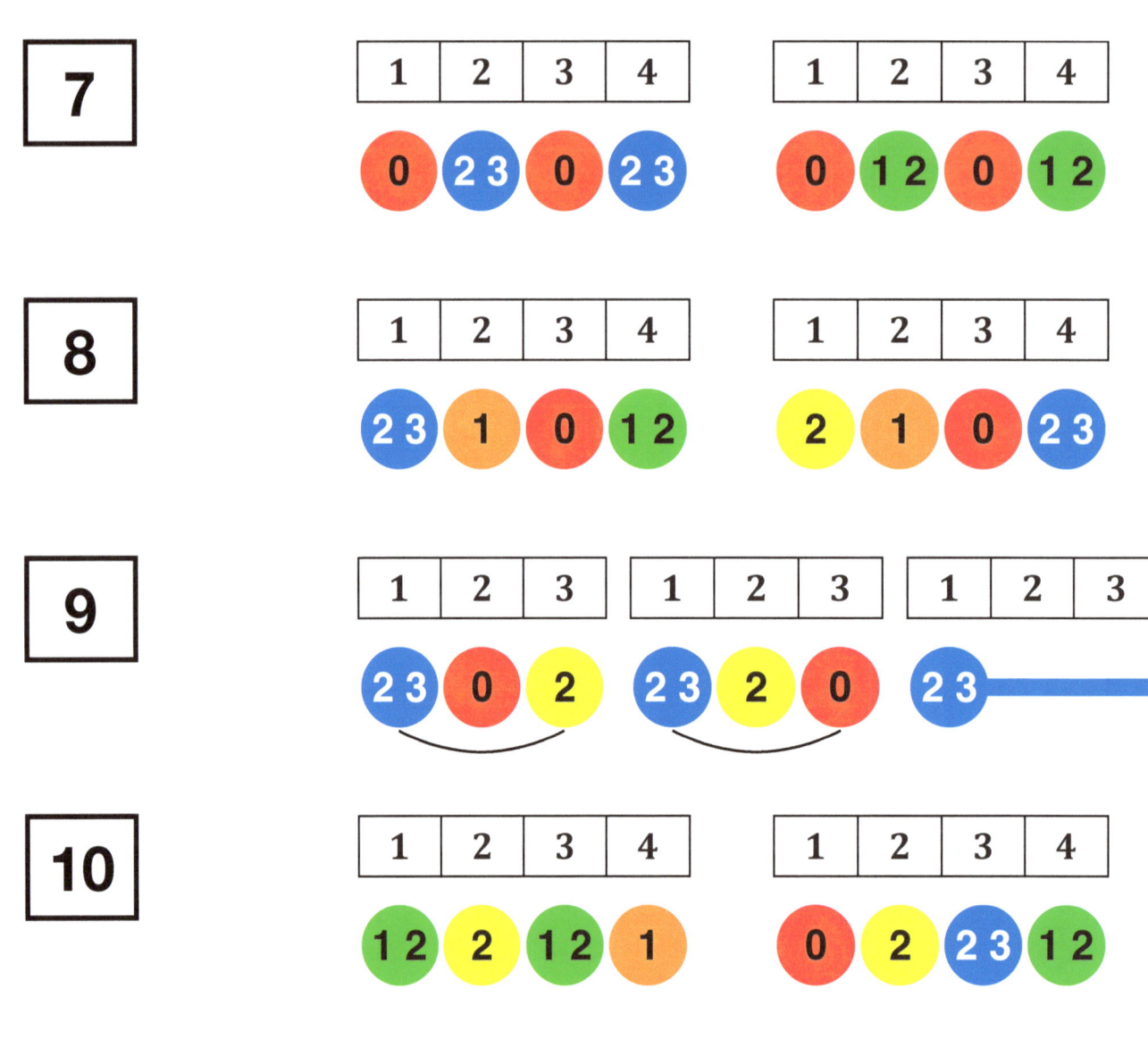

Technique Exercises 1

Play by Reading

Play the following exercises reading music notation.

 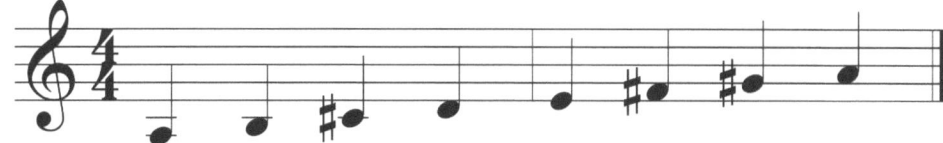

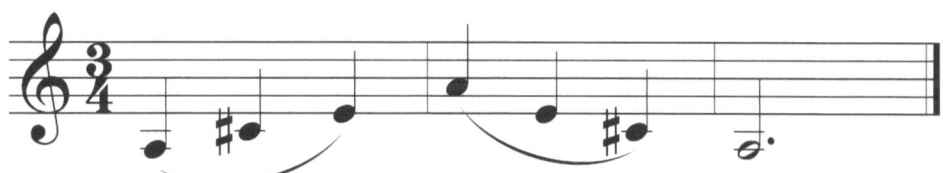

Technique Exercises 2

Play by Listening

Listen to the following exercises. Use the Color Fingerings to play what you hear.

12

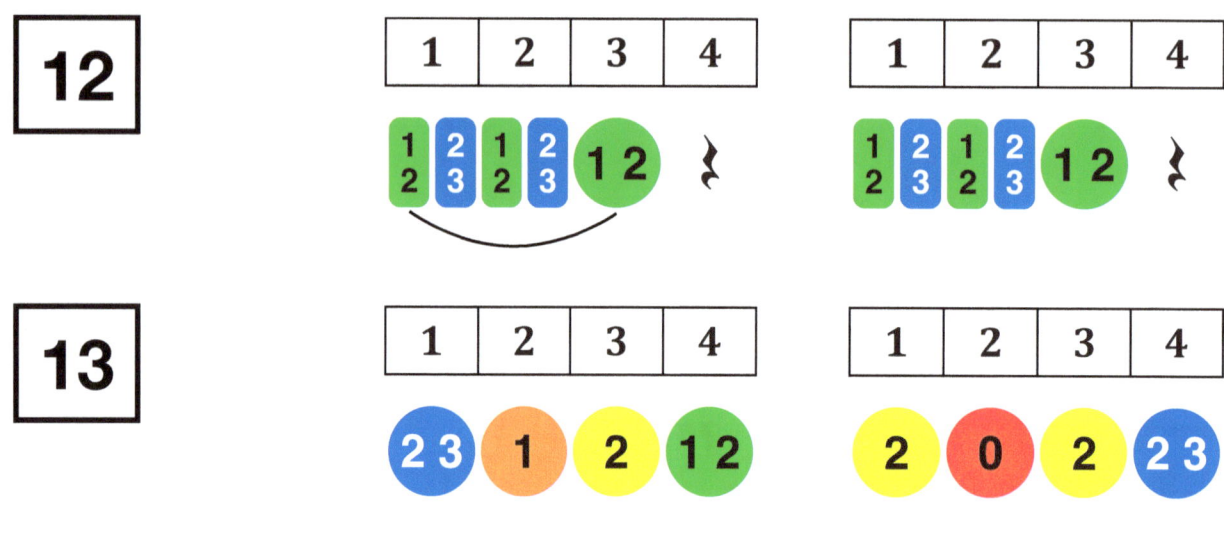

13

14

15

16

Technique Exercises 2

Play by Reading

Play the following exercises reading music notation.

Songs Group 1

Play by Listening

Listen to the following exercises. Use the Color Fingerings to play what you hear.

17 Waltz in A

18 Ah, Vous Dirai-je, Maman

Songs Group 1

Play by Reading

Play the following exercises reading music notation.

17 Waltz in A

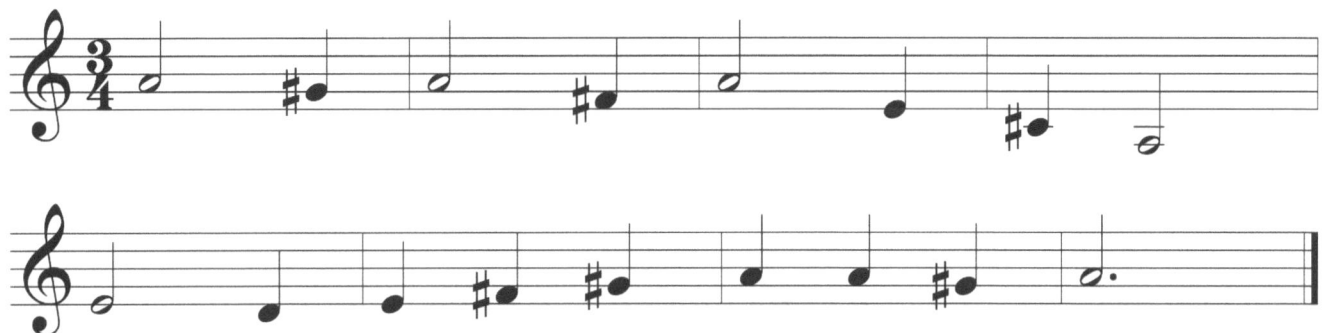

18 Ah, Vous Dirai-je, Maman

"Oh, Shall I Tell You, Mum"
18th Century French Folk Song

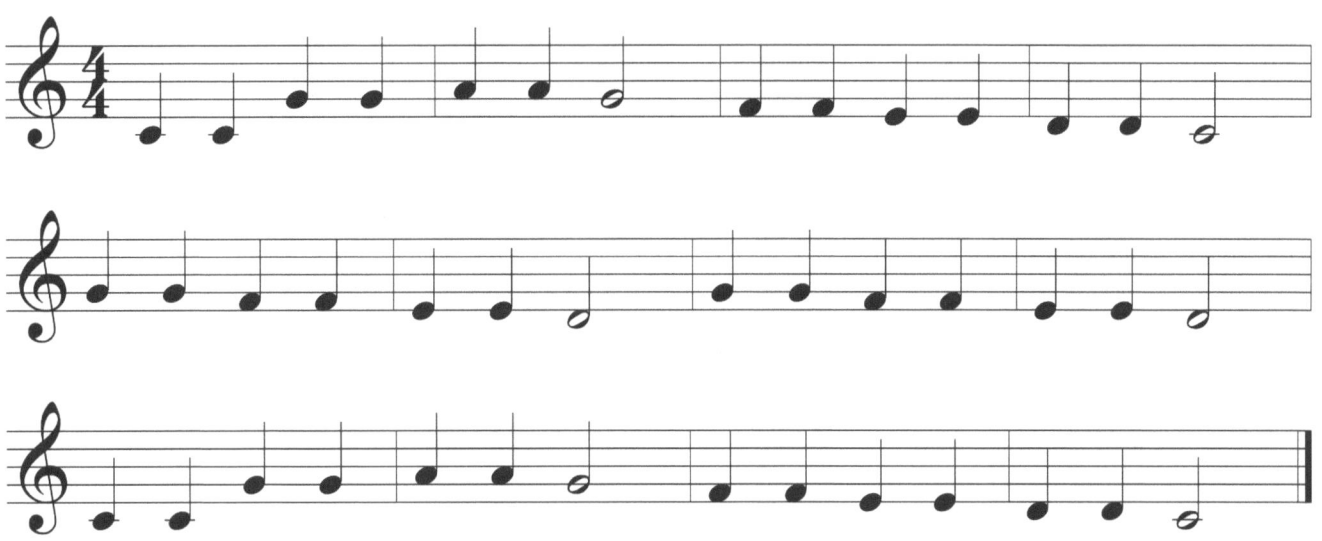

Brass in Color

Songs Group 2

Play by Listening

Listen to the following exercises. Use the Color Fingerings to play what you hear.

19 A♭ **Major Study**

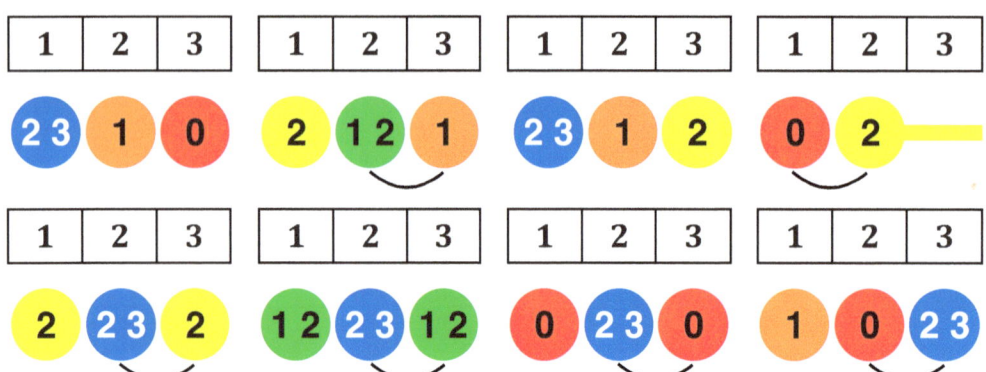

20 **Symphonic Melody**

Songs Group 2

Play by Reading

Play the following exercises reading music notation.

19 A♭ **Major Study**

20 **Symphonic Melody**

Johannes Brahms
Theme from Symphony No. 1

Lesson 3

1st Valve

For this fingering you press down the first valve. This is the fingering you use to play the notes **B♭/A♯** in the High Range. It is the same fingering you use to play the notes **F** and **D** in the Middle Range.

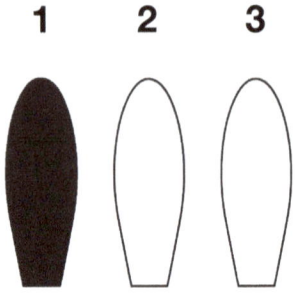

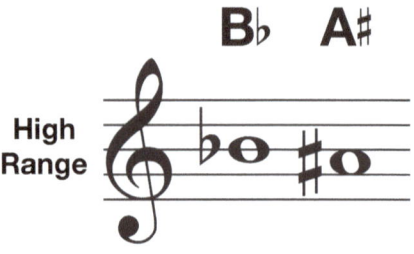

Play by Listening

Listen to the following exercises. Use the Color Fingerings to play what you hear.

21

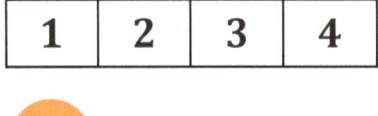
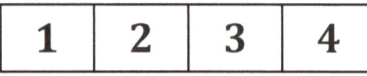

22

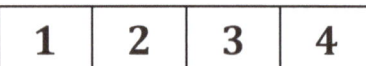

23

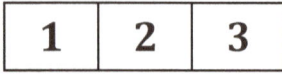

Lesson 3

Stem Direction

A note in music notation has three parts: the note head, the stem and the flag. When a note is written below the third line of the staff the stem of the note is on the right side of the note head and points up. When a note is written above the third line of the staff the stem is on the left side of the note head and points down. Notes written on the third line of the staff can point either up or down on the staff.

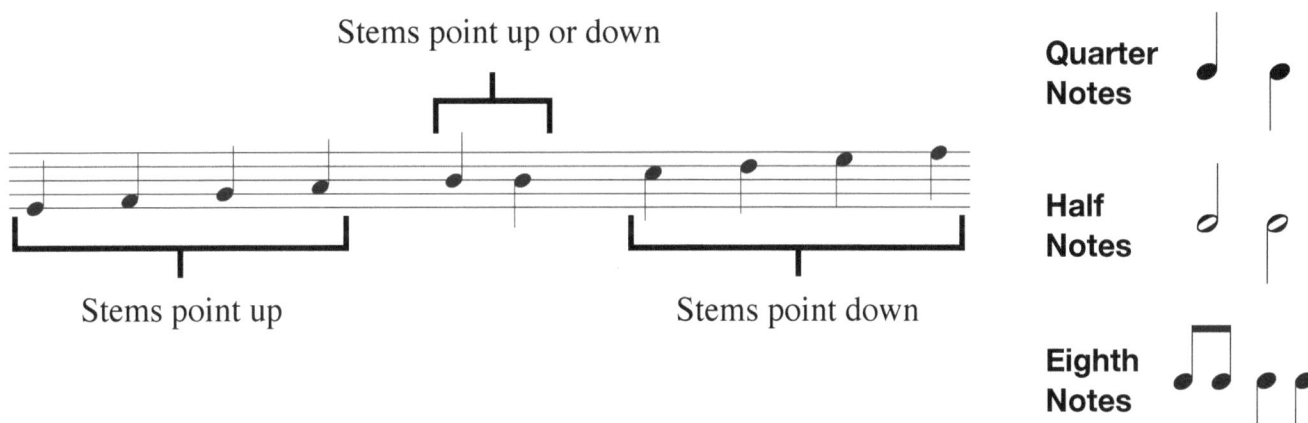

Play by Reading

Play the following exercises reading music notation.

* B♭ and A♯ are written differently, but they sound the same.

Brass in Color

Technique Exercises 3

Play by Listening

Listen to the following exercises. Use the Color Fingerings to play what you hear.

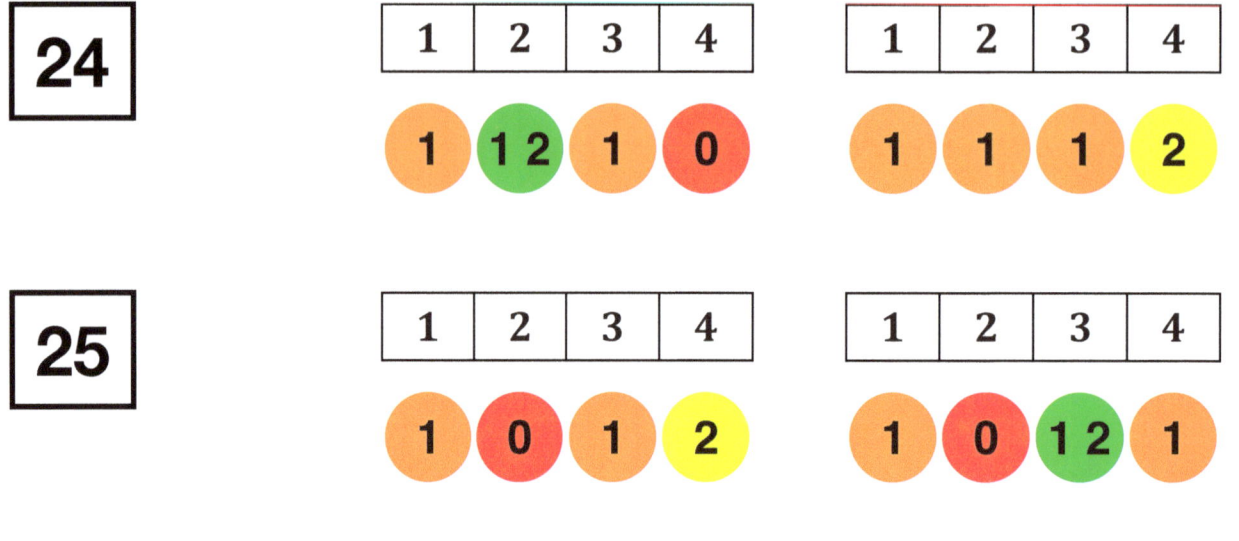

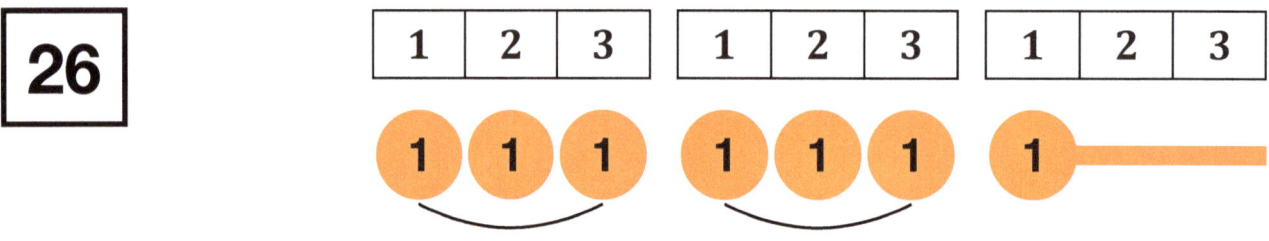

Technique Exercises 3

Play by Reading

Play the following exercises reading music notation.

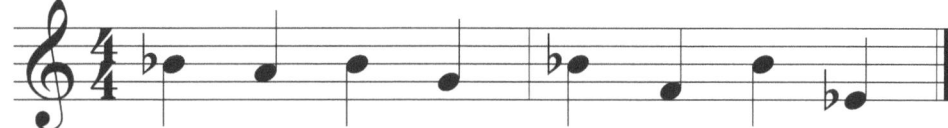

Songs Group 3

Play by Listening

Listen to the following exercises. Use the Color Fingerings to play what you hear.

29 Two Keys

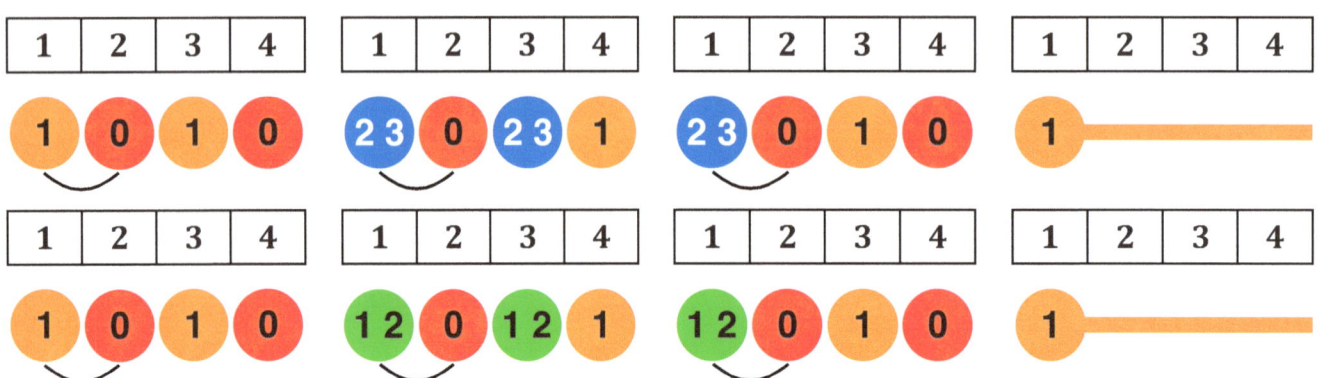

30 Stodola Pumpa

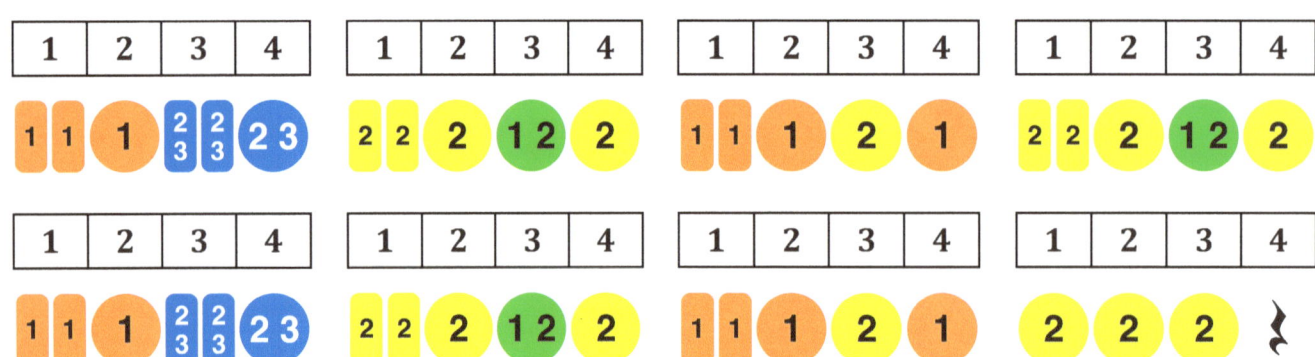

Songs Group 3

Play by Reading

Play the following exercises reading music notation.

29 **Two Keys**

30 **Stodola Pumpa**

"Barn Pump"
Czech Folk Song

Brass in Color

Songs Group 4

Play by Listening

Listen to the following exercises. Use the Color Fingerings to play what you hear.

31 Carnival of Venice

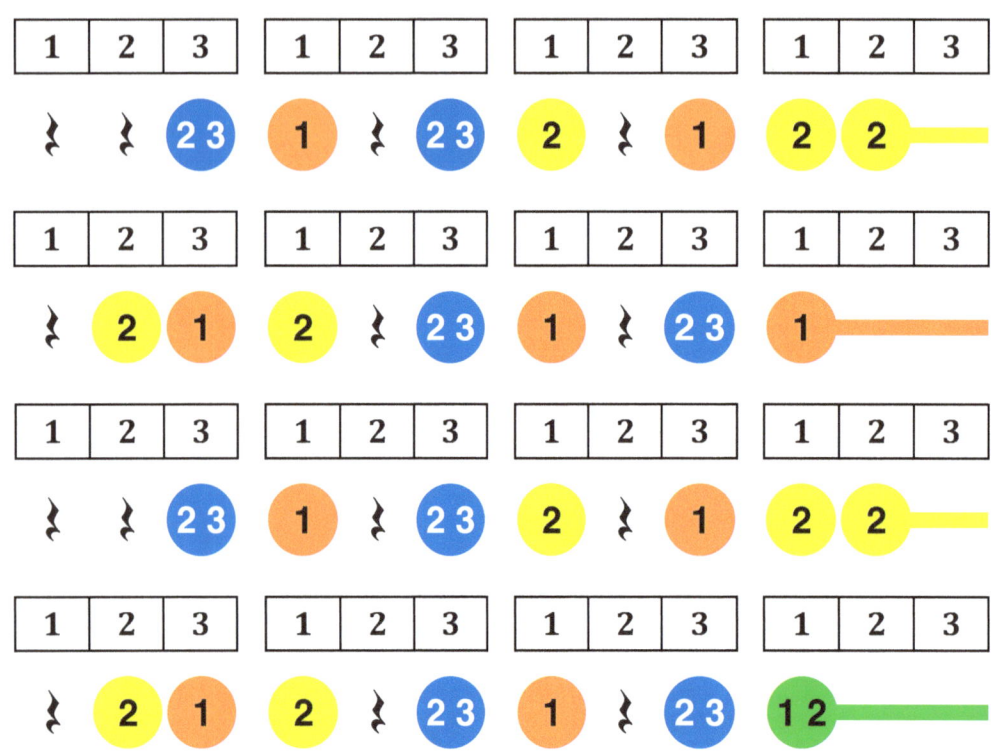

32 William Tell Overture

Songs Group 4

Play by Reading

Play the following exercises reading music notation.

31 **Carnival of Venice** Italian Folk Song

32 **William Tell Overture** Gioachino Rossini

Brass in Color 23

Lesson 4

2nd Valve

For this fingering you press down the second valve. This is the fingering you use to play the note **B** in the High Range. It is the same fingering you use to play the notes **G♭/F♯** and the notes **E♭/D♯** in the Middle Range.

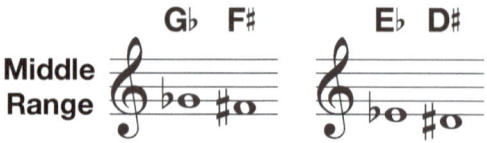

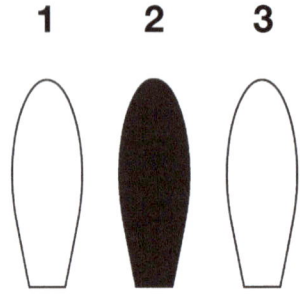

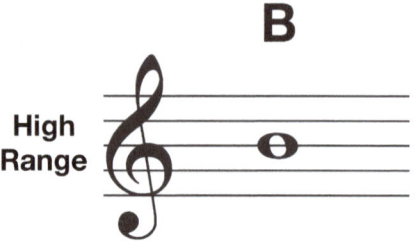

Play by Listening

Listen to the following exercises. Use the Color Fingerings to play what you hear.

33
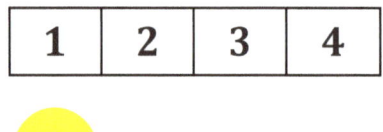
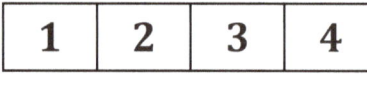

34

35
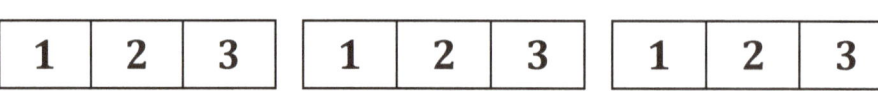
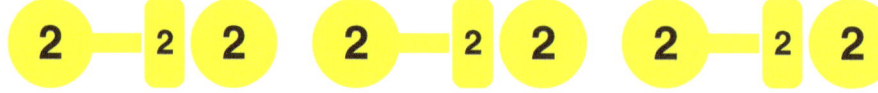

24   Brass in Color

Lesson 4

Dotted Quarter Note

When a dot (•) is added to a note it makes it longer by half when it is attached to the rhythm value (quarter note, half note or whole note). The diagram below shows a quarter note that represents 1 beat, and when a dot (•) is added to the quarter note it has a rhythm value of 1½ beats. This is called a **dotted quarter note**.

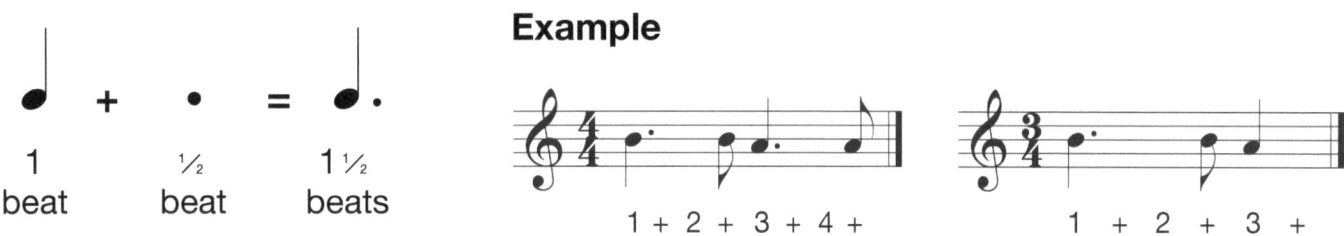

Play by Reading

Play the following exercises reading music notation.

Technique Exercises 4

Play by Listening

Listen to the following exercises. Use the Color Fingerings to play what you hear.

36
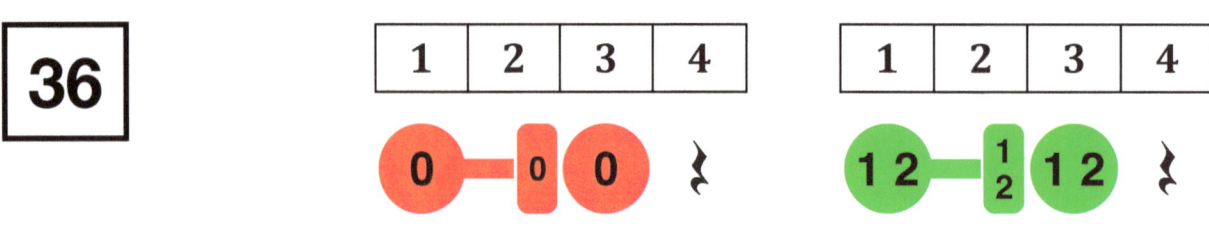

37
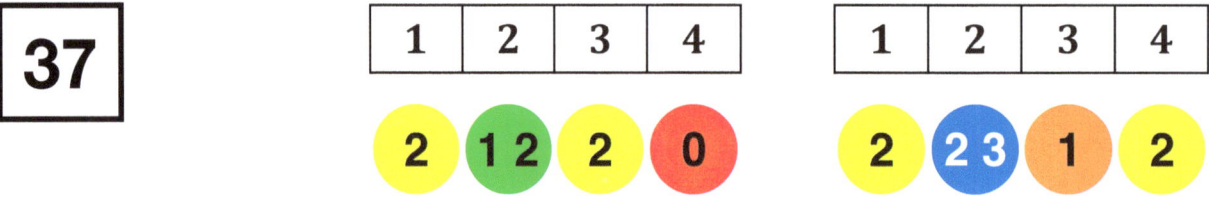

38
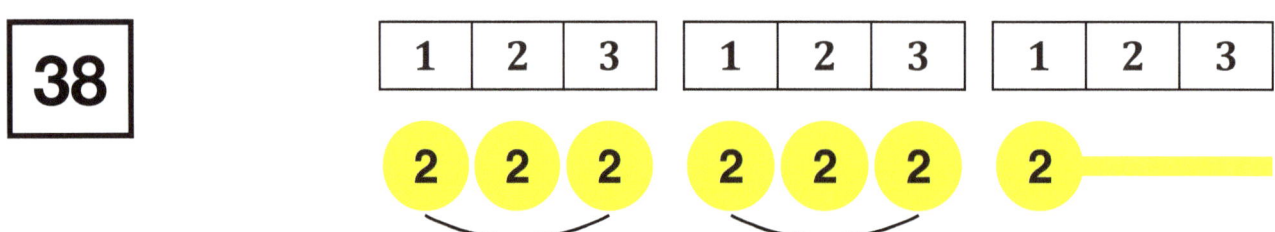

39
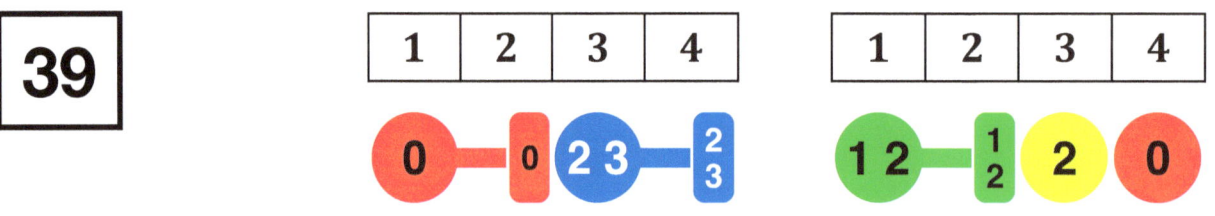

40
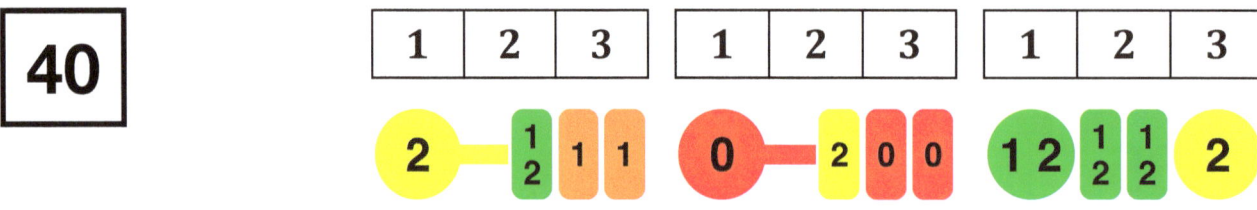

Technique Exercises 4

Play by Reading

Play the following exercises reading music notation.

 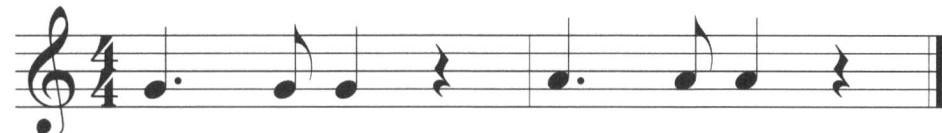

Songs Group 5

Play by Listening

Listen to the following exercises. Use the Color Fingerings to play what you hear.

41 Check the Dots

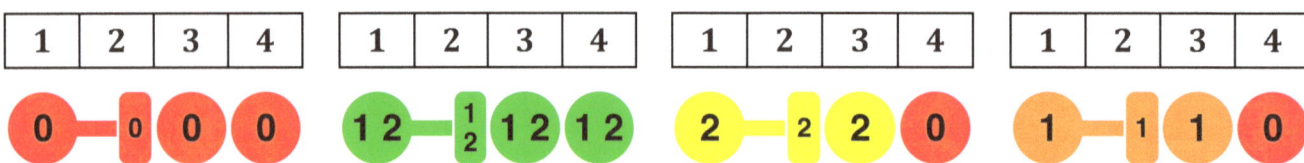

42 Alouette

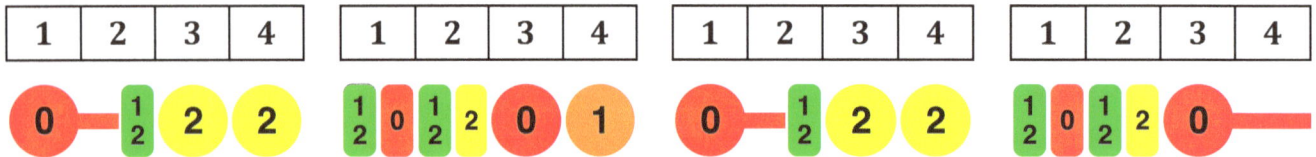

43 Chromatic Fanfare

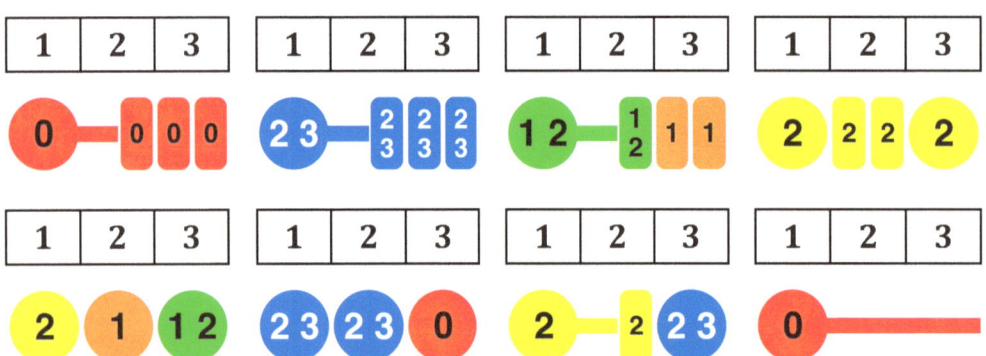

Songs Group 5

Play by Reading

Play the following exercises reading music notation.

41 **Check the Dots**

42 **Alouette**

"Little Skylark"
French-Canadian Folk Song

43 **Chromatic Fanfare**

Songs Group 6

Play by Listening

Listen to the following exercises. Use the Color Fingerings to play what you hear.

44 Berend Botje

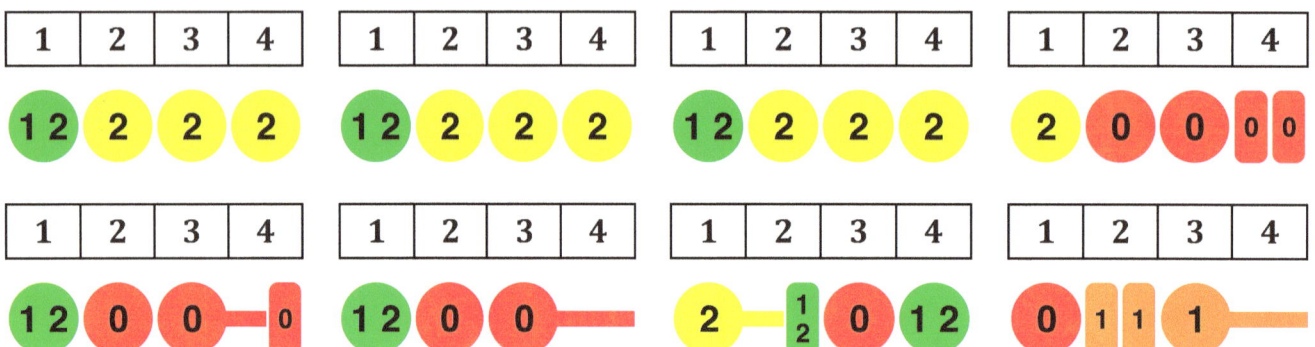

45 Abi Yo Yo

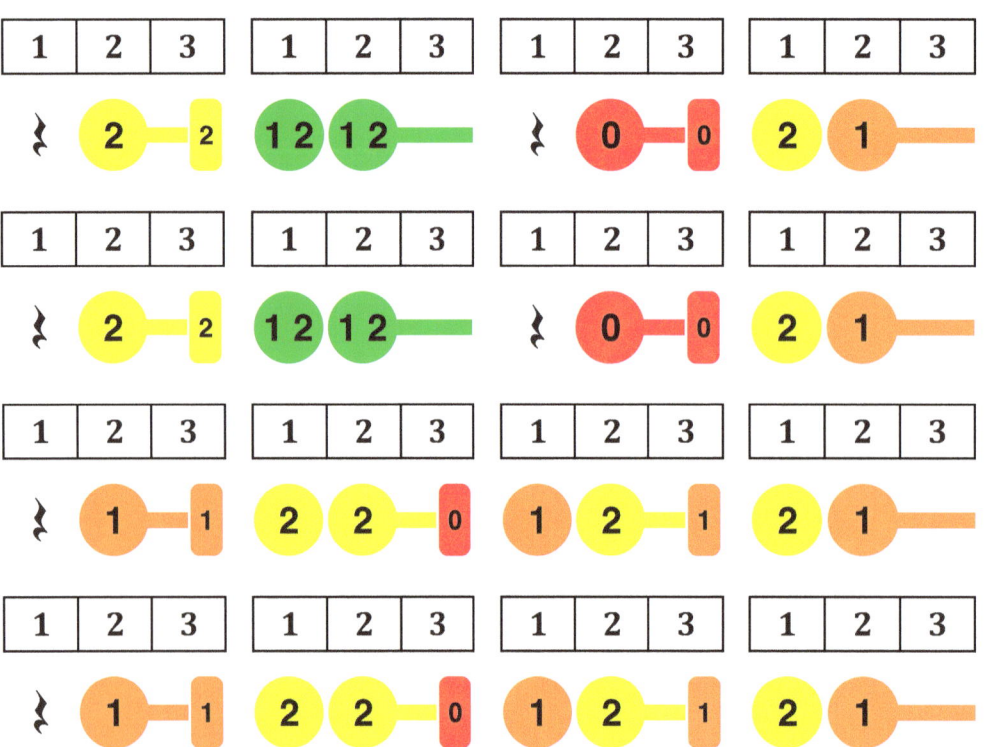

Songs Group 6

Play by Reading

Play the following exercises reading music notation.

44 **Berend Botje**   Dutch Folk Song

45 **Abi Yo Yo**   African Folk Song and Bantu Lullaby

Lesson 5

Open Fingering

For this fingering you do not press down any valves. This is the fingering you use to play the note **C** in the High Range. It is the same fingering you use to play the notes **G** and **E** in the Middle Range.

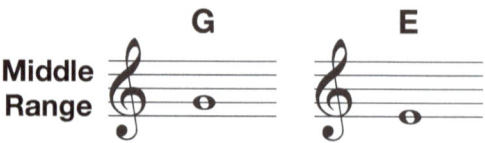

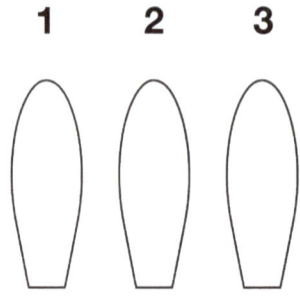      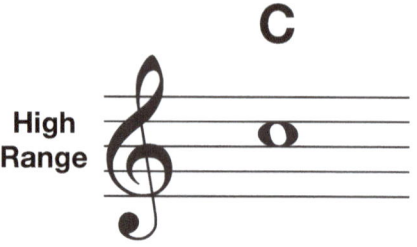

Play by Listening

Listen to the following exercises. Use the Color Fingerings to play what you hear.

46

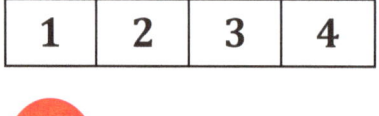   

47

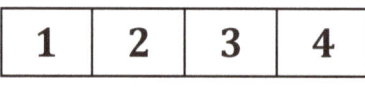   

48

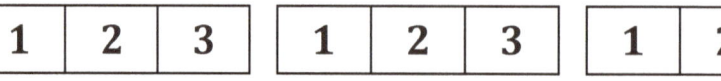

32   Brass in Color

Lesson 5

Harmonic Minor Scale

In French Horn Book Two you learned that scales are formed by using different combinations of half steps and whole steps. The pattern for the natural minor scale is **W-H-W-W-H-W-W**. To make the **harmonic minor scale** the 7th note of the natural minor scale is raised by one half step. The pattern of half steps and whole steps for the harmonic minor scale is: **W-H-W-W-H-W+H-H**.

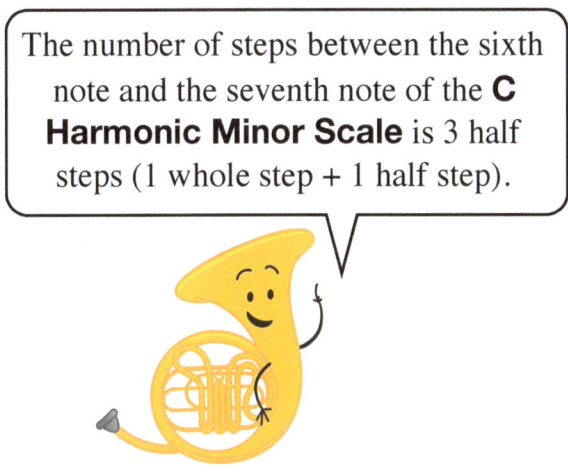

The number of steps between the sixth note and the seventh note of the **C Harmonic Minor Scale** is 3 half steps (1 whole step + 1 half step).

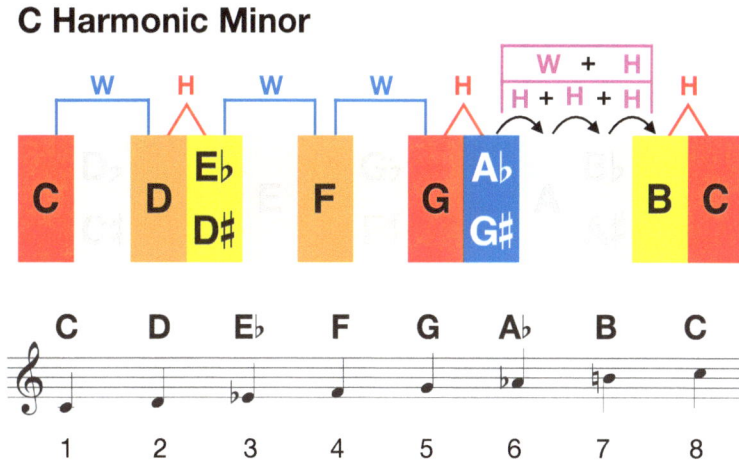

C Harmonic Minor

Play by Reading

Play the following exercises reading music notation.

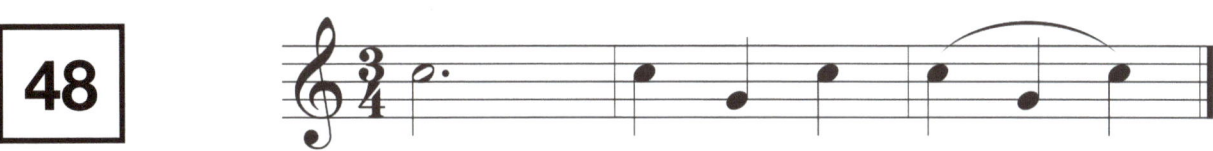

Technique Exercises 5

Play by Listening

Listen to the following exercises. Use the Color Fingerings to play what you hear.

49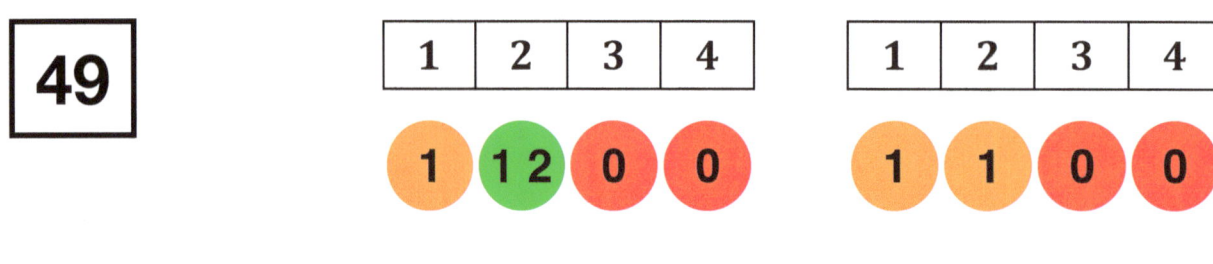

50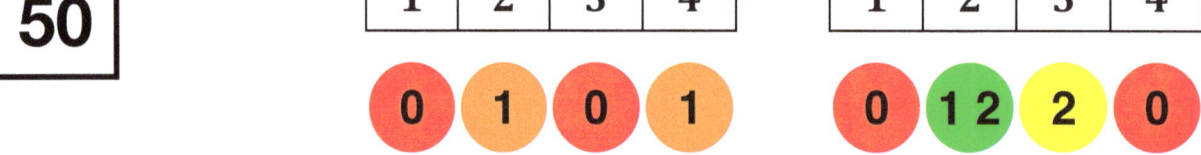

51

52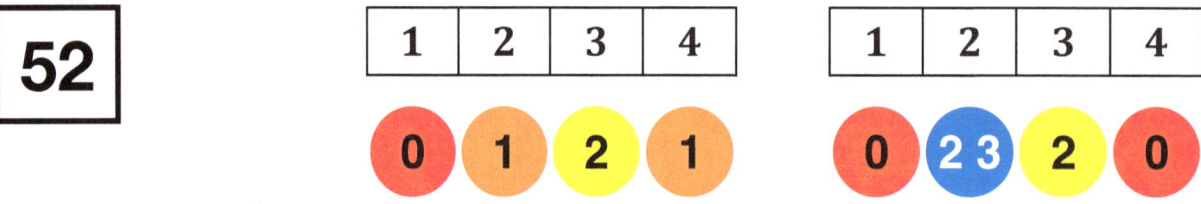

53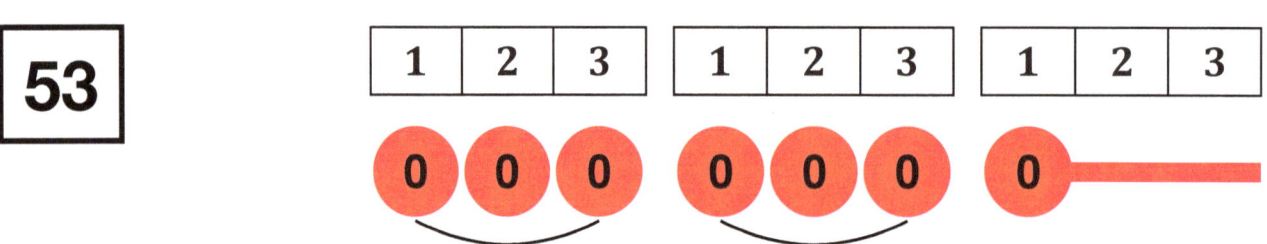

Technique Exercises 5

Play by Reading

Play the following exercises reading music notation.

 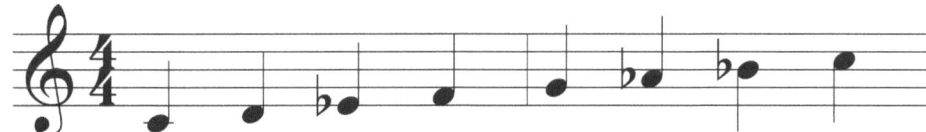

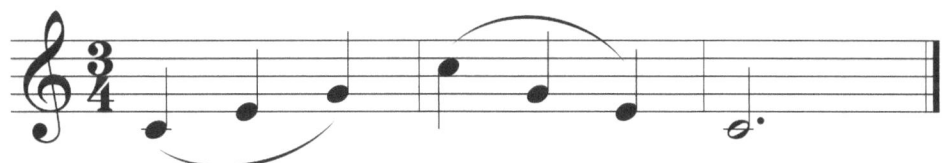

Brass in Color

Songs Group 7

Play by Listening

Listen to the following exercises. Use the Color Fingerings to play what you hear.

| 54 | **Minuet** |

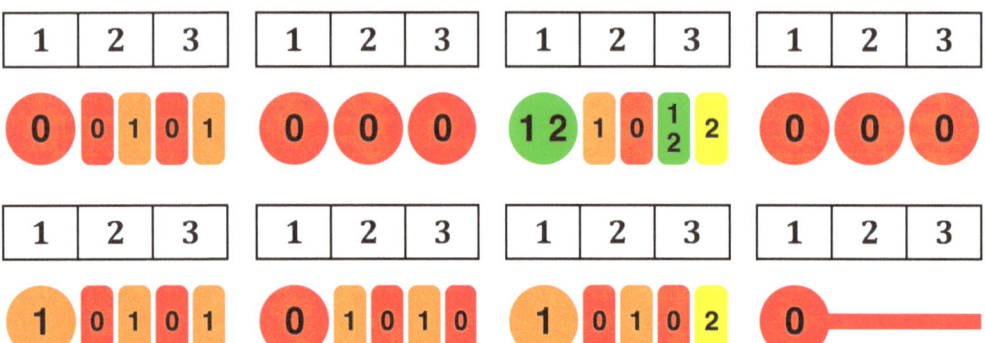

| 55 | **Mahler Tune** |

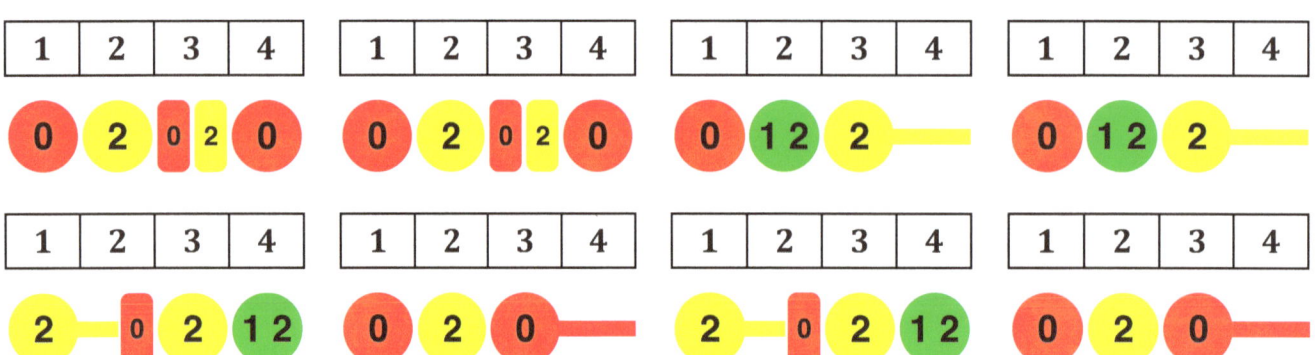

Songs Group 7

Play by Reading

Play the following exercises reading music notation.

54 Minuet

Christian Petzold

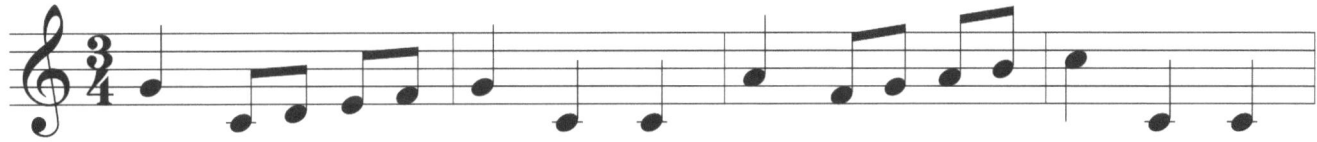

55 Mahler Tune

Gustav Mahler
Symphony No. 1, Movement 3

Songs Group 8

Play by Listening

Listen to the following exercises. Use the Color Fingerings to play what you hear.

56 Sea Shanty

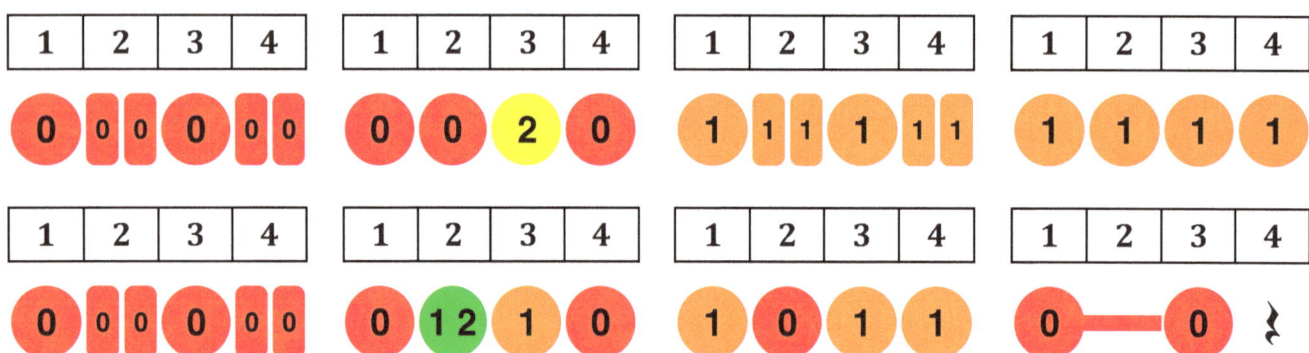

57 Momiji

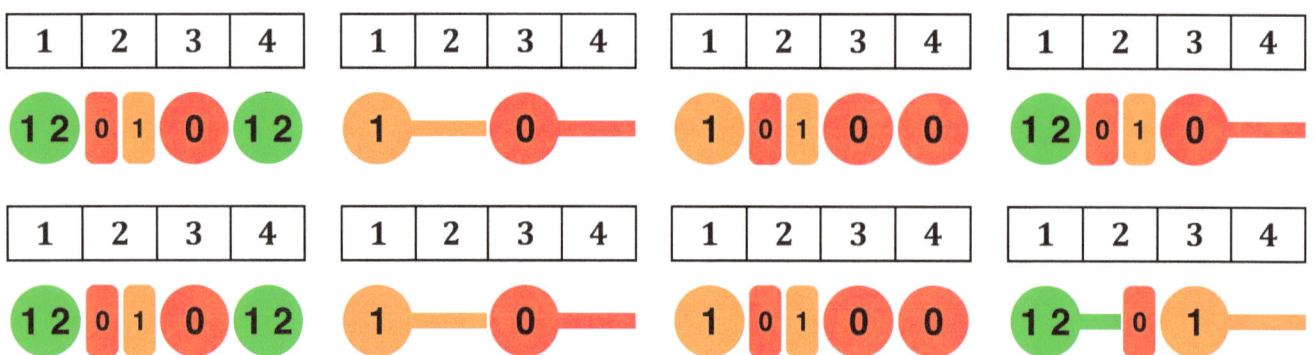

Songs Group 8

Play by Reading

Play the following exercises reading music notation.

56 **Sea Shanty**

57 **Momiji**

"Autumn Leaves"
Japanese Children's Song

Songs Group 9

Play by Listening

Listen to the following exercises. Use the Color Fingerings to play what you hear.

58 Hungarian Dance No. 5

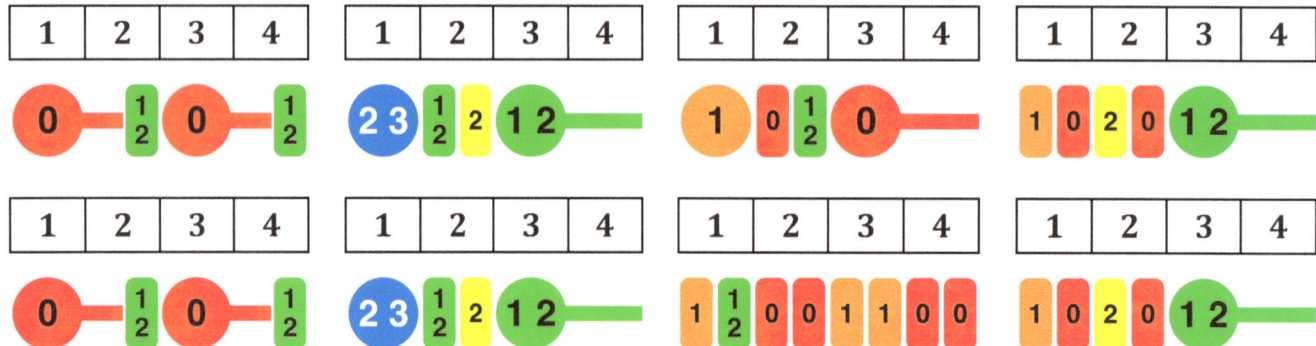

59 Arirang

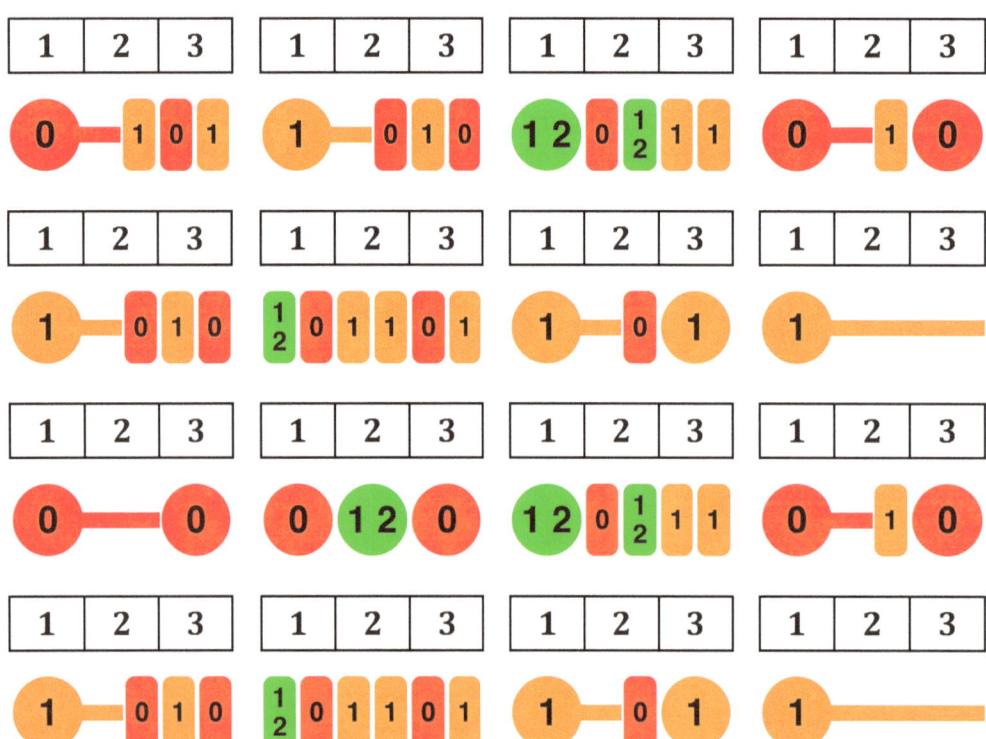

Songs Group 9

Play by Reading

Play the following exercises reading music notation.

58 **Hungarian Dance No. 5** Johannes Brahms

59 **Arirang** Korean Folk Song

Etudes

An **etude** (Fr., *étude*, "study") is a music exercise or a piece of music written for a solo instrument. Etudes focus on playing various music techniques and concepts. These etudes will test the knowledge and skills you have learned from the Brass in Color Beginner Method Series.

60 | Etude No. 1

61 | Etude No. 2

Etudes

62 | Etude No. 3

63 | Etude No. 4

Music Definitions and Symbols

Staff

Made up of 5 lines and 4 spaces. Music symbols are placed on and around the staff to indicate pitch, rhythm, dynamics and other instructions.

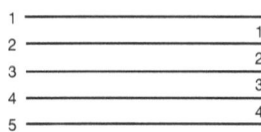

Time Signatures

Placed at the beginning of the staff. The top number will indicate how many beats are in a measure. The bottom number will tell you which rhythm value is placed on the beat.

4/4 Four beats in a measure. Quarter note gets the beat.

2/2 Two beats in a measure. Half note gets the beat.

Clefs

Clefs are placed at the beginning of the staff to indicate which notes are placed on the lines and spaces.

 **Treble Clef** - used for instruments that play notes that sound higher like the trumpet and French horn.

 Bass Clef - used for instruments that play notes that sound lower like the trombone, euphonium and tuba.

Treble Clef Notes

Pitch - how high or low a note sounds.

Note - the name of a pitch (Example: **G**, **F♯**, **E**).

Beat - the steady pulse in music.

Tempo - the speed of the beat (fast or slow).

Dynamics

Dynamics will tell you how loud or soft to play.

- *ff* **Fortissimo** - very loud
- *f* **Forte** - loud
- *mf* **Mezzo Forte** - half loud
- *mp* **Mezzo Piano** - half soft
- *p* **Piano** - soft
- *pp* **Pianissimo** - very soft

Accidentals

- ♭ **Flat** - lowers the note one half step.
- ♯ **Sharp** - raises the note one half step.
- ♮ **Natural** - cancels sharps and flats in a measure.

Rhythms

♪	**Eighth Note**	= 1/2 beat
♩	**Quarter Note**	= 1 beat
♩.	**Dotted Quarter Note**	= 1 1/2 beats
♪	**Half Note**	= 2 beats
♪.	**Dotted Half Note**	= 3 beats
o	**Whole Note**	= 4 beats

Brass in Color

Fingering Chart

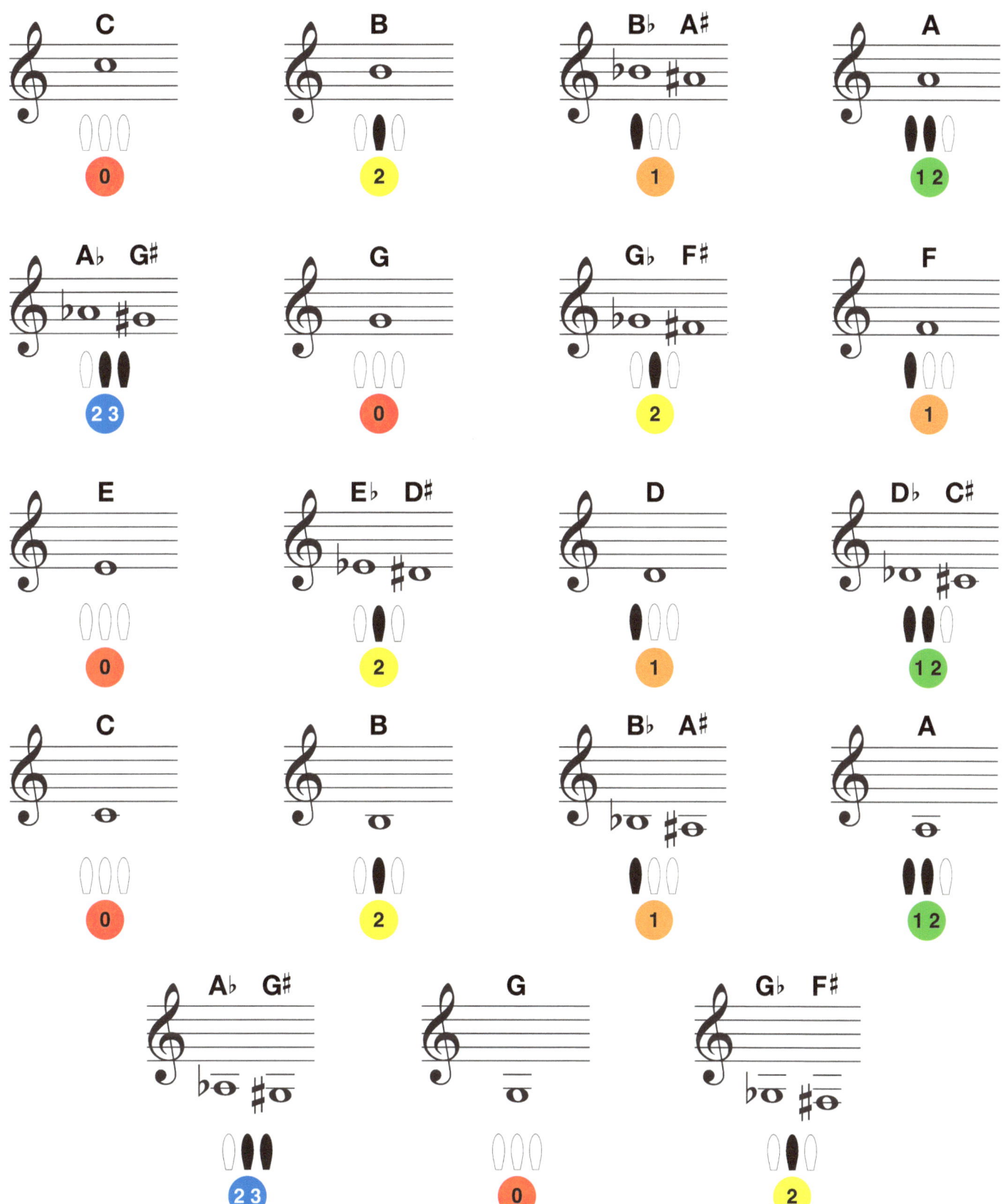

Brass in Color

Books

FRENCH HORN BOOK ONE will introduce notes of the Middle Range. Students will learn the basics of playing the French horn and also introductory music concepts.

FRENCH HORN BOOK TWO will introduce notes of the Low Range. Students will learn about slurs, eighth notes and scales.

FRENCH HORN BOOK THREE will introduce notes of the High Range. Students will learn about 3/4 time, dotted quarter notes, the harmonic minor scale and etudes.

www.ingramcontent.com/pod-product-compliance
Lightning Source LLC
Chambersburg PA
CBHW050748110526
44591CB00002B/14